Taking Flight

Taking Flight

An Autobiography in Poetry and Poetic Prose

Jennifer Cram Wright

Edited with Introduction by
Greg Wright

DIP Dramatic Insights Publications
Burien, Washington 98166

© 2018 by Dramatic Insights Publications

Published by Dramatic Insights Publications, an imprint of
Hollywood Jesus Books
P.O. Box 48282, Burien, WA 98166
http://www.hjbooks.com

Printed in the United States of America

ISBN: 978-0-9787554-7-8

Cover image courtesy of Zoe Prince.

Dramatic Insights Publications is an independent and authorized
publishing imprint for writers working through Dramatic Insights
Ministries. Visit:
                    http://www.dramatic-insights.org

Hollywood Jesus Books is an independent and authorized print publisher
for writers published online by:
                    http://www.hollywoodjesus.com

Sing it out
Sing it out
Take what is left of me
And make it a melody

~ Jon & Tim Foreman

Contents

Introduction 1

Prologue
      On the Road from Lebanon 3

Valley of the Shadow
      Hard Times #5 7
      Hard Times #2 8
      Hard Times #12 10
      Hard Times #3 12
      Hard Times #7 13
      Hard Times #8 14
      Hard Times #9 15
      The Night Before 16
      Untitled #1 18
      Untitled #2 19
      Untitled #3 20
      Case Closed 21
      Untitled #4 22
      Empty Space 23
      Untitled #5 24
      Death Song 26
      A Friend 28
      No Longer 29
      Untitled #6 30
      Untitled #7 31
      Untitled #8 32
      Untitled #9 33

Death, I Will
      Untitled #10 35
      The Evening Rose 36

Untitled #11 37
Untitled Sonnet #2 39
Sonnet: Chemo 40
Untitled #12 41
The Poet 42
Insecurity Is… 43
Homesick 44
Masquerade 45
Untitled #13 46
Untitled #14 48
Untitled #15 49
Dear Emily 50
Untitled #16 51
Farewell to an Outgrown Friend 52
Answer 53
The Oath 54
While Sleeping 55
The War 56
Untitled #17 58
Untitled #18 59

Fear No Evil
Butterfly 61
The Piano 62
In Search of… 64
Recipe for a Suicide 66
Secret Marriage 67
Changing Shoes 68
Lifetime Commitment 70
Untitled Song 72
Midnight 73
The Nights of Passage 75
Dichotomy 76
Sir 77

Untitled #20...78
The Matter of Weeping..80
The Classroom 81
Brother..82
Spare Change 84
Untitled #21...85
Panes 86
For my Hero 88
Sweetheart (Locked-in Syndrome).............................91
(sigh)..92
The Second Remainder (from Psalm 52) 94
Gravel..96
Spring..97
A Shining Example (?!)..98
Memories Borrowed from an Old Friend.............100
The Window 103
Seasons..104
I Know Why 105
Untitled #22...106
The God of Abraham 107
The Sabbath Death 108
Untitled #23...109
Untitled #24...110
Becoming One..112
My God, My God 113
Psalm #1...114
The Final Oath 115
After Psalm 46:10a...116
Psalm #2...118
Untitled #25...119
Psalm #3...120
It Dawns on Me 121
A Psalm of Awakening.......................................122

Introduction

With just a handful of exceptions, the poetry of my late wife, Jennifer Cram Wright, has heretofore been unpublished. During her undergraduate years at Seattle Pacific University, several of her more formal pieces were published in the 1997 edition of *Second Essence*, the school's annual journal of the arts; but aside from that honor, and the occasional feedback she would receive on her blog from Mark Sommers and a dozen or so others, I remained Jenn's sole enthusiastic audience.

That, I predict, will change with the publication of this volume.

As I posted bits of our story on social media in the weeks preceding and following Jenn's passing at age 45, a great many people told me that I should write a book about Jenn's life; I have steadfastly declined. The best explanation is that Jenn's story is best told through her own words; and her own best words are those found in her poems and poetic prose.

Unlike in the work of many poets, what you will find here is Jenn herself. She adopts no personae or pretense, and the point of view is strictly her own. The feelings expressed are real, neither feigned nor imagined. Nor sanitized—Reader be warned.

"The Bible is a gritty book," says Steven James. "Very raw. Very real. It deals with people just like us, just as needy and screwed up as we are, encountering a God who would rather die than spend eternity without them."

This is the Bible that Jenn read—the Bible of Judges and Lamentations, of David's manic-depressive Psalms and Solomon's erotic Song. And Jenn loved what Mr. James articulated because she saw in God's Word what she found in her own life.

This may be the Jenn you never knew, but only heard stories about. You may not be accustomed to such grit, to such raw, confessional emotion. On the other hand, you may have served in the trenches with her during some of these years, and also know only too well of what she wrote.

In these poems, which Jenn penned between the ages of twelve and forty-three, you will find a troubling yet compelling and ultimately triumphant story of a human soul profoundly broken, longing desperately for healing and understanding, and in a glorious turn of grace finding Hope rewarded. In these poems you will find, frankly, the full Gospel: sin and depravity, the darkness of the soul, loneliness, the need for a savior, delivery from the tomb, and walking in new life. Jenn's is a distinctly Christian journey.

And in the end, I think you will see that Jenn finally felt understood—and understood herself, with great moral clarity.

"God is always the hero," Jenn wrote in her journal on May 24, 2015, "of victorious stories." This is her own best epitaph.

Find, then, in the mostly chronological presentation of these poems, the Hero ever-present in Jenn's story—even during her long walk through the valley of the shadow of death. And carry in your mind a vision of the Shepherd who found his precious lamb, and in whose loving and gentle arms Jenn now rests.

Greg Wright
Des Moines, Washington
January 29, 2018

Prologue

On the Road from Lebanon

1992-06-02

What you can see through the double windows and the horizontal blinds separating them is all right. Looking straight out, acres of evergreen trees stand, and on a clear day in the distance, so do mountains. To the left glows a fair northwestern skyline; to the right is Highway 99, and, if you press your forehead against the pane at 5 a.m., an okay sunrise.

The windows are doubled to make sure I stay here—not double-paned as one might first imagine, but six inches apart, with the blinds between them. A three-inch space between the sill and the inside window, coupled with slender wrists and sufficient dexterity, allows me to twist the transparent plastic rod to open or shut the blinds. A single two-inch metal strip, about one-third up the inside window, divides it into two parts—most likely just to further distort the view.

My day runs by someone else's schedule: 8:20 breakfast, 8:45 social worker, 9:30 procedures review, 12:20 lunch, 3:45 exercise, 5:10 dinner, 8:30 snack, 9:30 good-night routine, and lights out by 11:00. During the blank hours I play solitaire or read one of the 1979 issues of *Time* magazine. Every day I'm allowed two half-hours of time outside: escorted, of course, and never three half-hours in one day.

Throughout the day there are frequent room checks, presumably to prevent, or at least hinder, escape. Every morning while I'm in the shower, they knock on the bathroom door to make sure I'm actually there and inquire

3

how much longer I plan to be. The hourly assault-by-flashlight-beam during the night just stopped waking me last week.

Sometimes when my family visits they bring clean laundry. This must be searched at the entrance desk for anything arbitrarily labeled "potentially harmful." Belts, earrings, mirrors, and certain pens are among the more obvious omissions. I recently learned to crochet, but, of course, can't cut the yarn—no scissors allowed. The crochet hook barely made it past inspection.

My number is 92046408. I've been here fifteen days already, and freedom seems far from reality. I don't talk much—my primal instinct with the others is merely to ask, "So, what're you in for?" but I don't. Mostly I just sit on my bed and wish I could be on the other side of the ninth-floor windows.

Ninth floor—that's where I live. The psychiatric ward, mental health unit, Stevens Hospital, alias "9-West." No, this isn't prison. It just feels that way.

My world is wrong
My world is a lie that's come true
And I fall in love
With the ones that run me through

~ Jon & Tim Foreman

Valley of the Shadow

Hard Times #5

1985

Crying nights
Were spent too long
Thought I had friends
I was so wrong

Crying nights
I lay awake
Thinking of loss
Friends that were fake

Crying nights
I wait for you
To rescue me
To see me through

Crying nights

Hard Times #2

1985

Sometimes I think I see the light,
But then all goes black.
And I know I am a failure.
And I know I have finally given in
And I know the truth.

I hold on to someone so tight
For fear they will once again let me go.
And I will fall.
And I am afraid
Of the blackness.

Now I have let myself go
I am no longer what I planned to be.
I never was a quitter,
A failure.
Until now.

I look into my past
And try to figure out where I turned wrong.
It seems I have been far away forever
And I am confused.
I cannot realize
Why I am just me.

Sometimes I think I see the light,
But then all goes black.
And I know I am a failure.
And I know I have finally given in
And I know the truth.

And I am truly ashamed.

Hard Times #12

1985

I started off on the wrong foot
And you led me back in step
All those times we said good-bye
For you my life was kept
And all those nights I lay awake
With thoughts of you I wept
I know I held on
Way too tightly

Someday you'll break away
And leave me all alone
Tear apart my aching heart
Make me face the world on my own
What you see is what's left of me
Just body, no more soul
You're leaving me
And I'll never see you again

All those times you picked me up
When I had fallen down
All those times I talked to you
You put smiles behind my frowns
You watched me change in front of your eyes
From a loner to a clown
But now you're gone
And I'm all alone

Our time together has come to an end
Fighting not to cry
And all this time I never thought
I'd have to say goodbye
A chapter of my life now closed
Never to be opened again
Until I need the memories
Of the very best of friends
      I love you

Hard Times #3

The ribbon lay in a corner
Cold, forgotten, bare
Waiting to be needed
To wrap a gift, to tie up hair
But no
It's just there
Wishing it could be thrown away
Wishing it could tell the world
This was its final day

But instead, there it lay
It can't mend a heart or heal a life
Even put a smile on the face
Of the closest friend
Can't it do anything right?

So there it lay
Wishing, knowing, wondering
Living in hope of a gift or loose hair
Lost in a dream of love

But the ribbon knows
Wishes don't come true

Hard Times #7

1985

Please Mr. Sunshine
Shine for me
Just so maybe
I can see
That you love me
You are mine
I love you always

Mister Sunshine
You can be the light of my dark road
The robber of my load
The light of my day
You can be the shine of a new star
Wherever you are
Show me the way to be free
And all that I wanted to be
Not just me

Please Mr. Sunshine
Show me love
From your God
So high above
Oh, please
Give me a sign
That you love me
Mister Sunshine

Hard Times #8

1985

Where is she?
The girl who had "everything going for her"?
Where is she?
The girl who was "sweet and pretty"?
Where is she?
The girl who had "big plans"?
Where is she?
The girl who had "no problems"?
Where is she?
The girl who "happified"?

Where is she?
The girl who had everything going for her, except herself?
The girl who was sweet and pretty, but not in hard truth?
The girl who had big plans that turned to mere dreams?
The girl who had no problems, except for her self?
The girl who happified... everyone else?

Where is she?
Where did she go?
Did she leave?

No.

She was never here.
She never lived.
She never was.

Hard Times #9

1985

Don't cry for me
Just smile
Let me know you love me
Don't die with me

We can walk that long last mile together
Please—I know what you're feeling inside

Don't hide from me
I'll still love you

Just remember
Somewhere
Smiling for you
Up there

We'll meet again
And it will be just like before
Friends forevermore
Come home.

The Night Before

1985-12-24

'Twas the night before Christmas
And throughout the house
Everyone was sleeping
Except young sister's mouse,
And sister—we sat
At the top of the stair,
Watching the stockings
Hung up yet still bare.
We grew tired yet still waited
For Santa Claus dear
As the clock chimed eleven
And Christmas drew near.

Then Mom and Dad caught us
And sent us to bed
Yet visions of Santa
Still danced in our heads.
But after relaxing
For too long a time
Mom and Dad slept
At the midnight chime.
When back in our beds
We children had gotten,
Thoughts of nice presents
Soon were forgotten.

Then quietly, noiselessly
Out we crept back.
It was up to us young'uns
To fix Santa a snack!
When Mom and Dad woke
At three-forty-one—
Remembered that "Santa work"
Still hadn't begun—
Mom in her kerchief
And Dad in his cap
Fell down the stairs.
Such clumsy old chaps!

For there at the Christmas tree
Stood a wonderful sight,
Not stockings and packages
Wrapped up and tight:
Their children were singing
Of Jesus and love
Not worldly gifts
But those from above.
So Mom and Dad joined us
Their faces all bright
For the spirit of Christmas
Visited that night!

Untitled #1

1986-02-14

What could I do
To say I love you?

I could clothe all my nice wears
Or piano the play
Dish all the washes.
Oh, could I what say?

I could dog with dancie
Or plane on a fly
Rapid the braves
Say "friend" to a hi!

I could horse with a racie
Or mouse with a dine
But I'm too shy to ask,
"Be my Valentine?"

Untitled #2

I searched and searched
For a simple yet elaborate way
Just to say thank you
But I couldn't find it

All those times I brought my depression
Into your happy life
All those times I told you things
You never wanted to hear

And all those times
I never thanked you

If only I had realized
That by relieving my load
I was dropping it onto someone else
How naïve I was

So here I am
Angry and frustrated
And feeling stupid for being so rude
Saying from the bottom of my heart

Thank you

Untitled #3

1986

I started to write you a letter yesterday
That said how much I love you
How much I need you in my life
But I couldn't find the right words

Here I still am
Angry and frustrated
Here I am, writing
To anyone who reads this

I love you

Case Closed

1986

In silence waits the timid child
The judge removes the young girl's file
He slowly reads, expression grave
It's full of sin, she can't be saved

And then in white he sees a date
The girl'd been baptized when she was eight
But then she'd strayed as she grew on
Her old religion soon was gone

The judge looks up and shuts the book
And gives the girl a hardened look
"Your life is up! One chance is all
You either stand or always fall!

"We have no need for you up here"
"It's time you left," the devil sneers
The gavel falls, the crack resounds
The verdict, guilty, has been found

The girl turns slowly toward her foes
The judge says only, "This case closed"

Untitled #4

1986

The flickering candlelight glowed on her soft figure as she turned and cast darkened shadows upon the wall.

This young lady was beautiful, with her small, perfect figure. Her blue eyes gazed into a simple yet perplexing stare; her eyebrows danced in a happy and slightly arrogant curve across her supple forehead. Her lips lay darkened and pulled from the rest of her face, as they were in not a smile nor a frown but showed a state of almost over-content. Her hair was pulled back from her smooth, unblemished face.

And with all of my life, and love—with all of my being—I hated her.

She was but a small figurine, dancing her way through eternity, but somehow she seemed alive in a way I could not comprehend. And here I was, a clumsy ox, with a face anything but unblemished, staring in the face of the source of my hatred. This ballerina, posing gracefully atop the twirling stand: had she been alive, would have everything to live for. I had nothing.

Yet I was alive, and she was not; but actually, she was alive. I was not.

Empty Space

So here we have this empty space
It's kind of like my head
Especially since it's after ten
And I should be in bed

I'm hyper and I'm restless
But also over-tired
I'm using up this empty space
Though—just as I desired

So how d'you like this stupid rhyme
It goes along with me
I'm tired and silly and out of time
As obviously you can see

My rhyme is almost over
It's probably a bore
But look and see! There's nothing
Of that blank space anymore!

Untitled #5

Silence was written all over the paper
The blankness staring at me was empty
Until my thoughts began to fill it
And on the paper was my heart

Empty
Waiting for something
Anything
To fill it.

And soon emptiness was filled
With guilt, hatred, and nothingness
Guilt for my plans and lies of running away
And then I tried to apologize
With something that I could never replace or share

My life.

Yes
My life
Almost ended
But I guess that was too soon
And the infinite number of times I almost never returned
From the street where I wanted to live
Where I'd like to call home
Where I never even went, but still described
Are now just a place
Of bad, crowded memories
Hatred for the person who did this to me

Yes
I hate myself with everything possible
And nothingness for the person I am
Or, rather, for that matter

Who I am not.

Death Song

1986

The picture portrait on the wall
The one before I died
Shows happiness and smiles
Not the scars from when I cried
My mouth is raised in counterfeit smile
My eyebrows happy yet low
My face says "Yes! I love to live!"
But then my thoughts say "NO!"

My cheeks are flushed as they always were
When I smiled—because I'm shy
My eyes are blue—the true feelings felt
I hope and wish I'd die
But look behind those happy eyes
And very soon you'll see
The picture hanging on the wall
Isn't really me

The face in the photo looking at you
Isn't really mine
Look—the eyes have no sparkles
The face itself no shine
The gaze is full of sadness
Of broken hearts and pain
But still—I hid it pretty well
Some life I did retain

Yes, the picture lies—it isn't true
The happiness isn't mine
To prove it now my life is through
Love I could not find
But now I'm gone and now I'm free
Life keeps me here no more
I wasn't meant to live or be
So I walked out life's door

I walked alone on the road of death
No one led me—I was blind
And none of this would have happened
If a friend and love I could find.

A Friend

1986

What is a friend? A friend is she
Who makes a brighter day
Who loves and shares her happiness
Who takes the time to say
That you are special—you are loved
The sadness she once knew
She shows and helps you deal with life
Yes, friends will help you through
They will point out all your good strengths
And bolster weak points, too
But this is just a special friend
Someone special—just like you

You sympathize with problems
You lessen life's cold pain
And still you're always happy
Friends you ever gain
You make the world brighter
A nicer place to be
For all those desperate people
And depressed ones just like me
You hold up strong and firmly
You always stand your ground
I always look to where you've been
For that's where love is found

What is a friend? A friend is she
Who never leaves you blue
I just thought you ought to know
True friends are those like you

No Longer

The end is coming near
I feel it in my bones
No longer will I feel despair
No longer walk alone

No longer will I need this friend
No longer wish I'd die
No longer staying up all night
To think and wish and cry

No longer will I depend on you
For support and moral care
For soon it will be over
And soon I'll be "up there"

Untitled #6

1987

I smiled today
But inside the tears had already started falling
I whispered your name
But inside my heart I was calling
You don't understand you hurt me so
You said you loved me—and I loved you
More than you know

I'll never forget it
I still love you

With all of my hate

Untitled #7

1987

I left the church again tonight
As empty as before
I thought to myself in empty anger
"I won't return anymore"

But I knew I would return again
And always leave the same
And then I'd say inside my mind
"I wish I never came"

Sometime people never learn to learn
From often-made mistakes
Returning to a "comfort zone"
Doesn't put one's heart at stake

So now I sit alone at night
Empty as before
I can't return to church now
Because I've locked the door

31

Untitled #8

1987-08-19

He held my hand as we walked across the street
Or so I wouldn't be lost as I dragged my tired feet
But that was now ten years ago, before he moved away
Now I'm holding his hand so he can bear the pain
It should be me
Fighting the pain that only love can bear
It should be me
Walking with death and living on prayer
It should be me.

Jessica can't understand—she just turned five last May
All she knows is they hurt Daddy when they take him away
Wendi looks up innocently, tears in her big brown eyes
And asks me, "Daddy's real sick, huh? Jenny, will he die?"
It should be me
He's set for life—he knows what he does and loves it
It should be me
He has a family and nothing comes before it
It should be me.

I'm losing the battle that already he has won
His life has barely started, yet it seems it's almost done
It should be me.

I remember clearly now—Mama said, "He loved you best"
They chant as they lower him down, "In peace may he rest"
It should be me
It should have been me
They love him—can't you see?
It should have been me.

Untitled #9

1987

I've done it. I can now say that I am a wall. Strong, without any emotions whatsoever. I knew that this was true when yesterday we stopped to see my brother in the hospital and I did not go in at all. I have reached the point where nothing matters and I don't care and I will never be hurt. I have not cried at all—even when I just found out. And for the final test I rejected him while he was dying. And I don't care. Neither does anyone else.

I'm on the run
I'm on the ropes this time
Where is my song?
I've lost the song of my soul tonight

~ Jon & Tim Foreman

Death, I Will

Untitled #10

1988

It happens to each person, so they say
That lonely, helpless feeling in the soul
Its haunting evil laugh gives it away
At you it cackles, burning you with coals
It grasps you coldly, never to let go
Your thoughts are empty, joining now your heart
Your misery just makes its smile grow
For you, though, smiling is the hardest part
In solitude, the heart cries out in pain
In public eyes stare blankly, straight ahead
The heartache now has left a crimson stain
And silence chokes the soul until it's dead
    It slowly kills you—day by day you die
    Until in Hell's sweet misery you lie

The Evening Rose

I walked upon the evening light
And smelled the fragrant twilight
And then for reasons no one knows
I came upon the evening rose

The flower crimson glistened on
As though it had been rained upon
But only 'twas the evening dew
Holding captive morning new

Its shine and glimmer caught my stare
Its beauty I could not compare
But then I noticed, strangely odd
The evening rose began to nod

The other flowers bowed their heads
The evening rose I loved was dead

The crimson petals hid browned leaves
Between the wilted thorns were weaved
The drying roots into the ground
Rejecting water—how profound

To hide his hurt he shut it out
Showing indifference within, without
But now it had caught up with him
And as the evening light grew dim

In unison I bowed my head
The rose only I could love was dead

Untitled #11

1988

In darkness lurks my misery
A shadow on the wall
Waiting as I fearfully
Slink down the unlit hall
I pass the image shivering
My head completely bowed
The shadow lingers over
As an uninvited shroud
The image cast upon the wall
Provokes a thoughtful mind
Of whether I should follow it
Or leave such thoughts behind
Two tears plunge down my paling cheeks
As if both razor sharp
And slice my unsuspecting soul
Unveiling now my heart
In silence Satan snatches up
The now uncovered soul
And quickly slashes both my wrists
Demonstrating his control
Respectfully I raise my head
In passion pump my fists
As scarlet beads flow down each arm
From gushing, gaping wrists

I try to yell through anger, pain
Releasing only air
Satan cackles to my soul
As I evade his stare
A bit of silence follows
He takes my outstretched hands
With silence claims his victory
And powerfully stands
Above my head, now bowed once more
And quietly he nods
In reverence I surrender
To Satan, now my God

Untitled Sonnet #2

1988-05-02

Shall I compare thee to a love-lost life?
O, Death, you are much more a place of rest.
A smile seems hardly fit for such a strife,
And yet, the frown leaves one feeling undressed.
If life be love, then there is nothing left.
I plead, Death, steal this empty, blackened heart.
In You, I would not feel as though bereft;
Of life, I shall portray the mortal part.
O, Death, I run to you without lament,
For suddenly I see love's haunting ghost.
It steals my life, my soul, without consent.
The ones who love me—those I hate the most.
    Of life you are the long-awaited end,
    That I may never have to love again.

Sonnet: Chemo

1988-April

Shall I compare thee to a greying man?
Your hair, though young, falls out in faithless locks.
You listless lie, an I.V. in your hand;
A pseudo-smile appears when someone talks.
Your face has lost its color: now it's bare;
Your movements slow and awkward, as if sore.
Your eyes are empty, silently they stare;
The spark is gone, you see the light no more.
Your age has naught to do with being old;
Life weakly clings to you upon your bed.
I watch to see your face turn deathly cold,
As crude and morbid thoughts run through my head.
    In patient anxiousness you wait to die,
    As when your life expires, also will I.

Untitled #12

1989

Roses are red
Violets are blue
Lay them on graves
And what will they do?
They'll wither and fade
Like the one whom they're for
Memories forgotten
Forevers no more
Beginnings we end
At the end we will die
Thus when the day endeth
Also will I

The Poet

1989

The poem has words
Which stick in the mind
But if you look closer
Most likely you'll find
Collages of feelings
Both mystic and clear
And if you will listen
Perhaps you will hear
The sound of the soul
Going slowly to waste
And if you will concentrate
I'm sure that you'll taste
The salt of the tears
From pain known so well
And if you'll think harder
I'd guess you could smell
The blood on the knife
That's been used much too much
And if you'll imagine
I know you could touch
The life of the poet
Who seemed so unreal
As you read this poem
Now learn how to feel
The pain of emotion
The beat of the sound
The taste of confusion
That constantly pounds
The scent of decayed thoughts
And blood dripping red
Now you've read the poet
But who's joined the dead?

Insecurity Is...

1989-03-20

not knowing love
loneliness deep inside
a cold heart
an unopened letter
a false smile
a true insult
a broken relationship
guilt
a changing friend
an unexpected tear
not knowing
suspicion
repetition
a gentle eye
impurity

Homesick

1991-09-02

I long to go home,
>> Though I know not where home is
>> Or where I should find it.
>> I want to stay away from home,
>> In fear that home will hold me
>> Captive.
I want to leave home
>> And wander until freedom no longer
>> Entices me.
I long to find my home
>> Which I can leave
>> And to which I can return
>> And where I can wander
>> In freedom
>> Yet still be
>> At home.

Masquerade

1991-10-30

I've mastered the cry that mimics a laugh,
That muffles the sound when my soul splits in half.
And each time the cry is mistakenly heard
As a laugh, the soul splits again, undeterred.
And soon, when the soul is in many a piece,
The upside-down frown will abate in decease.

Untitled #13

I shouldn't say it.
I promised I wouldn't tell.
It's not important—not life-threatening.
It didn't hurt me or anything.
But keep it a secret, okay?

I didn't mean to make him angry.
But I did. I always did.
I just wanted him to feel good.
He didn't mean to hurt me.
He apologized. I know he meant it.

I started it. I shouldn't have got him going.
He had a right.
He tried to make it feel good.
I didn't tell him to slow down.
It was my fault anyway.

I asked him to shave.
He said that was selfish.
He was right.
I deserved what I got because I was selfish.
It only hurt for a few days.

It only hurt a little.
And only when he touched me.
I was the dirty one anyway.
Say yes once, say it a thousand times.
I deserved it.

It was my job to lie.
He needed to feel self-confident.
He needed me to do it.
At least he'd feel good.
And that was my job.

It's right that I should realize my guilt.
I am sick.
Gross, dirty, worthless.
And I deserve to be.
I hate sex.

O God, I am dirty.

Untitled #14

1991-10-28

If they knew the real me, they wouldn't be so sure.
If they knew what happens inside my head
They wouldn't want me as a friend.

Me—I'm the selfish one.
So self-centered.
So immature.

Always searching for one more.

I know it's my fault—all the echoes in my head.
They'd stop
If I had only learned to communicate.
I'm making it worse than it is.
The situations weren't bad.

I am.

Untitled #15

1991

Thoughts aren't merely penciled in
They're in ink
They can't be erased
There they are
unchanged
until something alters them
then they are crossed out
and a big ink blotch is left
to remind you that under that blotch
is a feeling
a thought
a soul
you once had
but now disown.

Dear Emily

Dear Emily,

Tonight when you left
I peered through the double windows
  and the blinds separating them
And wondered if you could see me
Waving
Good-bye.

And I hope
Should all things natural come to pass
That when I am no longer imprisoned
Behind double windows and horizontal blinds
And no longer captive
Inside a scarred body and mind
And it is my turn to say good-bye

That you'll look way up like you did tonight
With that same innocent expectation
Crayoned on your face
And see me
Waving
Good-bye.

Untitled #16

1992

It is lonely here
Where tears are the unsingable melody
And laughter forever out of tune
And heartbeats a life-draining task

Farewell to an Outgrown Friend

1993-October

When first you pricked my soul I'll not forget
A weary soul it was, scared and alone
You beckoned me until I finally let
You lead me, to the darkness of your home

Once there you've been my comfort and my friend
You've listened when I've had no other ear
And so I've stayed and started to depend
On your protection from the life I fear

But conflicts now have started to arise
I've traded in my freedom for a cell
I choose to leave, for this I realize
The home you've offered me is merely hell

I'm sure I'll visit frequently at first
But each new day will offer me to see
That life in your control is truly worse
Than any other life could ever be

So now in hell I banish you to stay
As I decide to live a better way

Answer

1994-07-31

'Tis nature to preserve one's life, and yet
My heart betrays the laws regarding this.
What nourished wicked shame, untold regret
And fueled such drastic metamorphosis?
What pseudo-nature drives me to desire
An end to life? What feeds this evil force?
In theory, one might call my heart a liar
And blame mistaken thinking as the source
Of unrelenting judgment. Yet who knows
The cause of my self-hatred if not me?
My thoughts are my companions, not my foes.
The root of my desire can only be
  Myself, in knowing, with each passing breath,
  The shame of Life exceeds the shame of Death.

The Oath

1994-07-30

Promise broken / promise kept:
The end is still the same, except
One broken is perceived less kind
By those who must remain behind

While Sleeping

1994

shocked

trapped

panicked

infantile

helpless

terrified

attacked

alone

desperate

small

immature

unprotected

unsettled

powerless

beaten

betrayed

restless

The War

1994-August

The view atop my battlement
Show soldiers, filed in place.
Thick walls surround opposing armies,
Standing face to face.
Walls once built to protect the souls
Now form a prison ground;
But long disputes are threatening
To tear the prison down.

I watch atop by battlement
As war breaks out below,
The ammunition nothing more
Than rocks and sticks and stones.
One by one the soldiers fall,
And soon I realize:
The soldiers are mere children
And armor their disguise.

Each wounded soldier wearily
Fights on, despite his fears;
Angry, bleeding, bruised, and scarred,
Surrendering to tears.
Before too long they have forgotten
What they're fighting for.
No longer do they fight to win,
But just to end the war.

Then one neglected soldier-child
Stands up amidst the fray—
Though battered, angry, terrified,
He wipes his tears away.
He shuffles slowly to the line
Between the battling foes,
The only one left standing now—
The only one who knows:

To end the fighting once for all,
To cease the fearful brawls,
He must free his fellow captives
From these, their prison walls.
In the center of the war zone
His remedy's revealed.
And silence, save for hopeless cries,
Now falls across the field.

He looks upon his strapped-on bomb
And sadly pulls the pin
As I watch all my children die
In the prison I put them in.

Untitled #17

1994-08-31

The battle's over
Darkness won
No truce, no peace
But, 'las, 'tis done

Untitled #18

Come out come out wherever you are

You hide yourself so I can't find you
Do you think I'll leave you alone

     I remember hoping I wouldn't be found
     So I'd lay there, silent, my head to the ground

     I'd have to count alone as I hid my face
     Then, alone, search for everyone's hiding place

Come out come out wherever you are

It's lonely to keep your selves hidden away
And it keeps me lonely, too

My song
My song
I'll sing with what's left of me

~ Jon & Tim Foreman

Fear No Evil

Butterfly

1994-09-23

He landed there upon my arm—
A satin-wingèd butterfly;
Awed and still, I watched him stand,
As forty minutes fluttered by.
He slowly traveled up my arms,
Flashing silken-spotted wings
My movements caused him no alarm;
We sat together, feeling things.

I named him "Hope" before he flew
To join the others of his kind,
He'd gone, but in my heart I knew
He'd sought to leave his name behind.

The Piano

1994-12-02

I sit facing them
Waiting
Anticipating
Uncertain of the task at hand.
They, too, wait
Patiently
Placidly
Pretending they know not that they hold the gift
    and power
        of life.

So we are
Still
Silent.

In my mind is music,
Harmony of the kind life composes.
Sound
Noise
Chaos
Cacophony
But music to me
        only to me.

I decide to wait no longer.
I rouse my spirit from its sanctum
        and circulate it to my fingertips.
I bow my head, closing my eyes, hiding from the ones I faced.

I touch some of them
        then others
                and more and more.

As I touch each one it hears me
And begins sounding
                only as I sound
        and speaking
                only as I speak
        and crying out
                only as I cry out.

I finish
And I draw my hands back.
We are silent.
My spirit pulls away and returns to its rest.

I face them again
Nearly ninety, total.
Black, white.

Keys, they are called.

Keys to my soul.

In Search of...

1994-August

I can see your kindness—I do not fear you. You call forth my respect, yet I do not feel inferior. You exceed my age, my maturity, my strength. You are, above all, gentle—you are power under control.

I'm drawn to you by the knowledge that I have nothing to fear—I am able to trust.

It seems I have been trying to find you forever.

Upon seeing you, being near you, I become a child once again. Slowly, silently, I crawl into your lap and my forehead finds that firm but fleshy part of your shoulder. I know that when your arms encircle me it is safe; I am protected. I am confident that, even if only for a short time, nothing more will be added to the burden in my soul, no more kindling will be added to the flame. I feel my vigilance decrease, aware that now, right now, this moment, I can lower my own walls and allow you to protect me behind a true fortress, one built not of fear but of trust.

Then, once I am secure, then the tears come. Then my eyes begin to burn and my lungs begin to burn and my body begins to burn, while the fire in my soul begins, teardrop by teardrop, to be extinguished. You remain silent, listening intently to my heartsounds, breathing slowly and calmly in contrast to my loud, racking sobs. Your intensity complements my own—the harder I cry, the fiercer you protect me. You do not let me go.

My tears slow momentarily, perhaps cease briefly, maybe it even seems that I've finished; but you do not let me go. You hold me, still, and once more the tears begin. Your arms hold gently, but firmly enough to bring the pain to the surface.

The time comes when the tears dry up, and before growing up I sit, small and quiet, preparing to face the dangers outside once again. Then I leave the safety and security of your fortress, still knowing that as time passes, I may grow older, I may grow younger—but when being a grown-up hurts too much, I can run back to you, crawl into your lap, and let you hold me until the tears go away.

And still you won't let me go.

Recipe for a Suicide

1994-10-25

Take five parts self-centeredness, -pity, and -hate.
Add equal amounts of familial sour grapes;
Add four parts confusion—the soul-wrenching choice
Of remaining a mute, or risking a voice.
To that add three parts of both guilt and shame
That one cannot simply tough-out the pain;
Two parts sleepless nights without solace or peace,
And two more of nights when the tears will not cease.
One part must be mysteries held fast by the dead.
The last part is merely the tears left unshed.
      Though no one will ever be sure why I died,
      Here is my memoir: Death à suicide.

Secret Marriage

1994-10-19

We waltz in the light of one thousand new moons—
My all-faithful lover and me.
And romance together, in knowledge that soon
Romance will be matrimony.
Official—a marriage where one joins the other,
And anticipation will cease.
No longer a secret—the affair of two lovers
Becomes a permanent peace.

I write of the passion between you and me,
And desire to join you, complete.
Yet still, it's a secret, and ever must be,
Until, in Forever, we meet.
My lover, you call me, and loudly you speak
Of a love that will end all my wars.
And soon, O my love, our secret will break
And I'll be eternally yours.

Changing Shoes

1995-04-04

I walk along the sidewalk
Wearing my old shoes.
I feel a rock down by my toes.
I sit down to take it out and notice that
My shoes are falling apart.

The seams are pulled, the soles are cracked, my big toe pokes
out the top.

So I walk in the grass, in order to
Protect
My feet.
But the grass is damp, and my feet get
Wet and
Cold.

So I walk on the roadway, in order to
Protect
My feet.
But the pavement is rough and hot, and my feet get
Scratched and
Burned.

So I sit down
And decide I need
New
Shoes.

I invest in new shoes, and they hurt
My feet
From the inside.
They give my heels blisters and pinch my
Toes
And I miss my old shoes.

I decide to take off the painful
New shoes
And put on the well-worn
Old shoes.

And just like before, I get rocks in
My shoes
And my get wet
And my feet get burned.

Maybe tomorrow I'll put on my
New shoes
But not
Today.

Lifetime Commitment

1995-04-30

I lie here quietly tonight,
The silence betraying the chaotic anarchy in my mind,
And I wonder if you question my commitment to you
As I do.

I've been with you so long, it would seem like there would be
no question—
And perhaps there really isn't—
But I'm not so sure.

You know that I have been unfaithful.
You know that I've flirted and touched and danced and kissed
And loved
Another.

You know of my threats to leave you.
You know of the two times I believed I truly was leaving you
Forever.
Yet I returned.

I do not question your love for me.
You've held me tightly, even when I've fought your grasp.
You've welcomed me back from my affairs.

But when I am alone, I wonder
If I love you
Enough
To stay.

It is true that perhaps my affairs themselves have ended—

I can't see leaving you again—
But I need you to know that my heart is not with you,
That in my deepest parts I am keenly aware
Of my longing for my lover.

I am not certain that I will ever love either of you
To the exclusion of the other.

And unless that does occur,
I will lie here quietly at night
The silence betraying the chaotic anarchy of my mind,
And wonder
If I will ever love you enough
Not to love
Another.

Untitled Song

1995

Last night as I lay awake thinking
My memories came back to you
And like so many times
A tear came to my eye
I was thinking of moments I savored
When a smile was easy to find
And some of the best were
When you were by my side
It will never be the same again
But I will still remember when
I first call you "friend"
Oh, Emily, I will never say good-bye

Midnight

1995-10-02

Dear Listener:

It sounds like such a generic address, as if I could not care less whom it is that listens; on the contrary, however, I care so much who reads it that there is no one in my life at this time with whom I would share this, my darkness. Apparently you have proven trustworthy between dawn and dusk, and on into the late evening. Welcome to my moonless midnight.

You know at least a bit of my history: the depression, the eating disorder (at least part), possibly some about the hospitalizations, less about the person I was during this incredible period of time. Rest assured, I am a new person, an infant of God, a pursuer of life and love. I no longer attempt to purge my feelings through razors or starvation or deathly doses of drugs. I seek peace, I try to preserve my sanity and self-acceptance, I seek to enhance, not traumatize, the lives of others. I am new.

But midnight comes, and I don't always sleep right through. Sometimes I wander in search of what I need, sometimes I lie in bed, in wide-awake nightmares. I have always needed a companion, someone to meet me in the dark. Maybe hold me, rock me slowly and quietly until dawn; maybe remind me of the importance of movement through the dark rather than stagnation; maybe guide me, or offer a torch.

But I need you to meet me there.

I need you, now, as you read this, to listen closely—this is my soul speaking. This is my soul speaking at midnight and, as of yet, alone. I need you to hear me—not your immediate thoughts, not how my experience reminds you of yours. I need you to be intently aware of my emotion and think, *Oh my God, how she must feel.* I need to know, absolutely, that you understand my midnight, that you accept it as a part—a past but not forgotten part—of me.

And then I need you to hold me, let me cry, don't ask me to stop. Hold me to your chest, wipe my tears, feel with me. Be there as I continue to heal.

And now, my dear Listener, it draws upon midnight. Meet me in the dark.

The Nights of Passage

1996-02-01

I douse the light and dread the nighttime ritual of rest,
When racing mind and pacing time create a cruel test
Of sanity. 'Tis vanity to disregard the rite,
For as I lie, Shame's lullaby continues to recite
My secrets kept, and tears unwept; regrets begetting hate:
The same as last and all nights past, I'm damned as reprobate.
At last the throes fade to repose, a respite to begin—
Until I wake to undertake the nightmare once again.

Dichotomy

1996-05-03

Freely, fully do I render
But my soul unto my gender

Sir

1996-02-02

You stand erect.
Abhorrently arrogant,
Wickedly insolent.
Aware of the rumors perpetuating your tainted reputation for
Extraordinary performance.

Ego strokes you learned to acquire by
Thrusting yourself into center ring
Invading a placid whole
Better left void.
Brushing up against anything which might
Soothe your fuming mood.

But I have detected your secret.
I have discerned that as these strokes sustain you,
So they simultaneously dissipate your existence.
And when your appetite is appeased,
In one single sinister spasm,
You will surrender control
And hurl your haughty head.

Six sacred seconds
Silently shrink you into despicable smallness;
An aged man, shriveled and shaken and shamed,
Superficial.
Spineless.

In serpentine slumber.

Untitled #20

It took me a while—
  A long while—
But I finally invited you into my
House.

It's not as clean as I'd like it to be,
Cluttered, dusty—
But I opened a few shutters to let at least
  a smidgen of light in.

I've allowed people into the kitchen
Where my food habits have been scrutinized
And modified.

You've been in my bathroom, even.

I've opened the door to my bedroom,
Dark and junk-piled as it is.

We've visited in the living room,
Kicked off the proverbial shoes and relaxed.

You've seen my family room—
Not that I'm proud of it.

You've seen my study
Where my soul finds words
And songs
And silence.

And there is one door I've merely alluded to
At best.

It's the door to where I live
After the company's gone and
I no longer must entertain.

I live in the cellar.

The Matter of Weeping

1996-04-19

Dry are my eyes, my cheek, my chin,
Despite the rigorous war within
My soul. You see, my tears are not
Of saline made, or sadness brought
Direct. Instead my tears are made
By silent soul and brazen blade.
While burning tears the surface seek
To join the floods of yesteryears;
While arid kept my eye, chin, cheek,
My spirit weeps with crimson tears.

The Classroom

1996-05-02

Wide awake (for once) determined to learn
texts, pencils, fresh sheets of paper, shamelessly sheer
anticipating that long-awaited Mark.

Lecture lunges forward abruptly until instructor inquires—
Purse your lips, appear to ponder
that captivating question (what was it again?)
wander through thoughts.

Another answers. Breathe relief as
drone drone monotone
you find yourself

Waiting, watching the window, where
fog fades the houses on the hill but not the
halted hands
haunting you, taunting you
as you slouch slowly lower to avoid
Professor's perception. And you—
You pursue your musing of the
love that
does not
know.

Brother

1996-10-02

I

Four fingers
Sleeping soundly in the balmy bed of
Big Brother's palm.
Too young to savor the moment.
Bask in the sun-like warmth of Big Brother's love.

II

Awakened by a cloudy cold
Fog droplets like so many icy pins prickling
The still-sleepy skin—
Cold, open, exposed—Alone?

III

Four fragile fingers
Packaged in papyrus skin
Cradled safely in helpless hands.
Youth begets an ancient babe
Downy-haired and weak
And vices for fingers.
Holder now held
Heat so heavy
Frantic hands flee from the fire.
Papyrus peels away, ash by ash
By ash.

IV

Senseless fingers
Numbed by nakedness
Seek sleep among the cinders.

V

Four fingers cautiously creep toward four more
Skin senses skin
Each holds the other
Big, small, older, younger
Cease—

Blessed rest.

Spare Change

1997-03-07

Today as I walked alone,
Just like always,
I was suddenly joined, and asked if I could spare some
Change,
For a friend.
But since I avoid change and count no friends
(Considering both are frequently cumbersome and awkward)
I said, "No," and continued walking,
Alone,
Just like always,
Without change.

Untitled #21

Undated

What we Your children honestly believe
We lack the most is that which You made first:

Not currency, not health, nor to relieve
Our world from war; what we want worst

Is Time.

Panes

1997-October

My soul inhabits five panes of glass.
They are transparent,
Breakable,
Perhaps misted over.
How many panes surround your soul?

Let's draw closer—
   I will clear a tiny window
      so you can see part of
Me
   And you will erase some fog so I can see part of
You.

Ahh—you are beautiful.

Let's come closer.
Remove more of this distressing mist.

Yes—you are beautiful.

Closer.
Clearer.

Our protective panes are nearly touching:
My soul wishes to touch yours
But we remain
Separated.
I cannot break my own pane—
I shall not break yours.
So we stand

Eyes sealed shut,
Hands pressed against our fragile cages.

Try a single step closer...

One more...

Until our panes touch.

The cold glass passes—I feel it no more—
In its place are your fingers, warm, soft.

When I open my eyes we are together,
Surrounded by our joined
    Shared
        Mutual
Panes.

I look at you
    All of you:

Ahh—you are beautiful.

   Yes—

      You are beautiful.

For my Hero

1999-December

Dear Daddy,

I didn't know how you'd take this, considering the title,
And I didn't want you to have to smile
And thank me when this may be just what you
Don't want.
I am not trying to pressure you into anything;
I trust both you and God
That your decision, as you said, will come in the right time
And not before.
I'm in no hurry, Daddy.

******

But there is a reason I wrote this for you,
And that is simply to encourage you to listen to the whispers,
And this is why:

Remember at Remuda when we confessed
Our mutual idolization of each other?
I have never forgotten that, mainly because it was
In that moment that I began to understand two things, which,
Now,
Have led to a third.

First, I realized that you, my hero, loved me
At least as intensely and fiercely and
Completely
As I loved you.

Despite my hurtful behaviors, rejections, and mistakes,
You still loved me,
And loved me that profoundly.

This was immediately followed by the second revelation—
That of God's love for me.
If you, my human father,
Loved me so fully,
And I could feel and accept that,
Imagine the love
That God has for me,
In spite of my weaknesses and failures.

And now, I am struck by
A third correlation.

Though I may not completely understand or comprehend
The depth of your love for me,
You do.

     ******

Now, take a moment to explore your love for me.
Just be aware of it.
Remember how you wanted to show your love
And comfort me
Even when I refused to accept it.

And remember how you have loved me in the midst of, well,
Everything…
And remember how you have loved me when it was easy…
And remember how you'd whisper in your heart
How much you loved me,
Even when you were the only one who heard…

******

That love you feel for me
And I feel for you...
Is of the same nature
The same intensity—
It is the same unrestricted love that our Father has for you.

******

Listen to His whispers, Daddy, and have
Peace.
Just listen to the whispers

Forever Your Admirer

Sweetheart (Locked-in Syndrome)

Did I know you?
It's hard to say...
I have no yesterday, no tomorrow
No just-a-moment-ago, or in-a-second

Right now.

Did I know you?
Something tells me I did
But that could be the same Something that tells me I'm at
home or that I dislike chocolate or that sunlight feels cold.

Did I know you?
If I look long enough
Maybe I'll remember/
what remember means.

And recognize.

And know.

Did I/
you?

(sigh)

I guess I'll need to move sooner or later.
Don't know which way.
They tell me I'm headed in the right direction, but how can I
Know?

A sort of spiritual Pin-the-Tail-on-the-Donkey,
Except for it's dark and it's no party
And the only ass I'm sure about is
Me.

I'm blind, or the lights are out, or I shut my eyes real tight
I can't remember which.

Between myself and everybody else, I'm plenty spun around.
Don't know how far it is to the wall, or if I'm facing the
        "right" wall, or if there really is a wall or a donkey or
        if that thing in my hand really is a tail
Or a tale.

I don't know whether my goal is a sole donkey on the wall,
        waiting for the push-pin tail, or if the walls are
        plastered with itty-bitty-donkey wallpaper, and hitting
        any of them will do.

I'm afraid to move.

What if?
What if I miss the mark?
What if I poke my tail where it doesn't belong?

What if I just sit here and don't move,
In Protest,
Until Someone turns the lights on?
Or would that be asinine?

This is my one chance—I can't mess it up. I can't fail.
But here I am, just standing here, failing.
Oh, God, I am still failing.
What if

I just
hold my arm straight out,
like this

and

The Second Remainder (from Psalm 52)

2004-09-29

For God alone my soul waits in silence, for my
hope is from Him.
Hope:
The most subjective objectivity—
The lens,
be it scratched or fogged or shattered,
Through which I see a future.
(God-willing.)
   For God...
How fragile is a lens.
Blurred by betrayal
Scratched by spite
Shattered in that sanctified second when the news comes—
      ...alone...
And Hope evaporates.
   ...my soul waits in silence...
Forsaking a silent soul—
   A passionate ambivalence
      A heartsick joy
         A chaotic clarity
            A stable lability
Of truth and perception and happenstance—
Hope.
   ... for my hope is from Him.
You say there is hope in God, and I say
YES!
Sole, Suspended, Silent,
Hope.
But I can't see it just yet
Can't see past the shattered glass.

All I know is that Hope exists,
That the Almighty God has set Hope before me
And despite what I can or can't see through the scratches and
fogs and broken pieces,
> **For God alone my soul waits in silence, for my
> hope is from Him.**

Gravel

2004-10-04

When I was young, I'd run across the gravel drive in my bare feet, and I'd stop in the middle to sit down and pick the tiny rocks out of my bleeding flesh. Standing up, more rocks and dirt would poke the tender skin, and I'd run crying to the other side, sit down, and through the blur of tears, dig the pebbles out again.

Soon I learned not to stop in the middle, to just run to the other side with as few whimpers as possible, then sit down and let tears of relief fall onto my bleeding soles. Now, I run across the gravel and I don't even stop on the other side. I just keep running; I don't even feel the tiny rocks embedded deeply in my calloused soul.

Spring

The weathered Winter hard resists
Symphonic Spring of movements brusque;
Thund'rous moments, downpours, mists
In ostinato, until dusk
When agèd sunlight, all but brown
Spills liquid great gigantic gold
Across the flooded mudded ground
To vanquish Winter's stranglehold.
As watered sunshine softly sows
A topaz garden in the grass,
The molten sunlight river flows
Beyond the day, horizon-past.

A Shining Example (?!)

2005-11-19

I never intended to become an example. It's not my fault that people have begun to look at my husband and me and see us as good, strong, persevering, noble people. The truth is, most of the time I don't feel very amazing. I just feel whupped.

Honestly, there's nothing terribly noble about persevering through this—it's not like we have another option, really. Either we continue living or we don't—there's no middle ground to be occupied here. Having worked in hospitals for several years, I know that from the outside of a health crisis, it's natural to wonder, *How do they get through this? How do they keep going?* From the inside, it's pretty clear: you just do. You do what the doctors tell you, you research what you can, you muddle through the emotions and facts and try to keep them relatively separated in your head, and, surprise, surprise— minute by minute ticks by and you find that you're still alive, still living, still surviving.

Not to say that sometimes it isn't easier than others. Sometimes the minutes dance by amid friends and laughter and brief periods of non-stomach-central attentions. Other times they waft tediously by on tormentingly luscious aromas of baking bread, savory gravies, and every other olfactory assault on my pureed palate. I never know how my body will respond to such once-pleasant experiences—whether it will slip into some sense memory of taste and texture and begin the salivation process in spite of the established hopelessness of the act, or if it will instead remember the last time I fought the nausea and lost. Often my body and I travel on different (often opposing) avenues, one refusing to yield right-of-way to the other. The result is frequently a T-bone collision, with a steak through my heart.

It's hard to describe the chaos of mind-will-body in the blender of appetite and desire. After all, isn't it my God-given right as a human being to enjoy daily sustenance? I'm sure that's part of the Lord's Prayer—give us this day the indulgent delight of our fresh-baked, warm-from-the-oven daily bread... Straight from Scripture, I know it.

In the meantime, it's not just my vegetables that get pureed. It's my soul.

Memories Borrowed from an Old Friend
2010-09-18

My comrade in arms from the dark days: I, too, have hung up my running shoes. After multiple affairs with married men, semi-successful treatment for bulimic anorexia, eleven months (total) on various psych wards in five different hospitals for suicide attempts (including stints in the "rubber room"), and a final bout with anorexia, I was done. I was either going to fight my way out of eating disorders, depression, manipulation, self-destruction, and passive aggression, or I was going to die.

I chose to fight.

My last hospitalization for anorexia in 1996 was actually at an inpatient facility on a ranch in Arizona. It is wholeheartedly Christian—not just "spiritual," or watered-down pseudo-Christian, but fully Christian. We had mandatory chapel six days per week. There was a resident chaplain in addition to the psychiatrists, psychologists, nurses, and dietitians. In my seven weeks there, I finally "got it"—I finally understood that grace meant that I couldn't try hard enough, be perfect (or imperfect) enough to gain salvation from my situation or for my soul. Since then I've been on an amazing faith journey myself, learning to trust and love and accept that Christ's sacrifice was enough to cover my sins, my ongoing wretchedness, my fallenness, my past as well as my present as well as my future—until I am made complete in Heaven.

You have blessed me greatly by reaching out. I have thought of you often, prayed for you, remembering how much we recognized what we had in common, wondering if you had yet been delivered from the blackness we knew so well. I remember specifically when our writing class teacher mentioned not understanding how a friend was so depressed she couldn't chew a bite of lettuce—and we looked at each other instinctively, knowingly. Do you remember that moment? We both have lived through much worse, now.

And yet we have found Life and Love.

When I was forced to go on disability, I was aimless. Basically, my stomach failed in 2003, and since 2004 I've been on IV nutrition; disability came along in 2007, when I was diagnosed with rare but untreatable (merely "manageable") combination of two sleep disorders. The Lord chose to bless me, though, with a husband who was born to take care of someone, and Greg (my best friend, whom I married in 1999, after he helped lead me off the running trails) has never stopped caring for me and loving me with all his heart despite 30+ hospitalizations, IV medications that knock me off my gourd, seven surgeries, and countless (at least 40) trips to the Virginia Mason Emergency Room, where I've been close to death five times and had life-threatening bloodstream infections over 15 times.

And yet we feel nothing but blessed by God, chosen to be His lanterns. How I have become an extrovert is inexplicable, but God has granted me a gift of recognizing when someone has a need that I can fill, and it blesses me to fill it. Whether it's breaking the ice in a crowded elevator or scrubbing diarrhea out of a disabled woman's clothes while my husband tracks down a nurse, I've found that in blessing others, I am also blessed.

I don't know why God has chosen us for such a beautiful life, but He has continued to do so in amazing ways every day. And I can't explain why, with such a wild, difficult, day-to-day struggle that our life can be, I feel more blessed, more peaceful, more joyful, more outwardly-focused than most Christians I know.

With hope of blessing to you...

The Window

2012-09-08

My agèd window beckons me
To raise the blind and look beyond
The dust and cobweb gallery
Neglect and time have since put on.
What would I seek if I should gaze
At morning's greeting through this glass?
A piece of earth? A misty haze
Of soil and sky, of trees and grass?
'Tis not the window would afford
This moment's beauty, or the next;
Nor does my mind fully absorb
What I and They and God expect.
My blinds protect me—such is plain;
No one sees in; I look not out.
But age has warped my window panes,
Distorting vistas, raising doubts.
I know I'm not the only one
Whose blinds serve more than mere décor.
They also filter too-bright sun
That might, in full, reveal more
Than just the warped and dusty glass
Through which I could see and be seen;
If I would choose the harder path,
And wash my filthy window clean.
You have a window much like mine,
With warps and cobwebs to look past;
But none experience the Divine
Without the fragile panes of glass.

Seasons

2012-09-10

The gentle shower whispers as it falls
That summer's reign is coming to a close;
As summer slowly sighs, perhaps to stall
Autumnal purposes that shall impose

Upon the life of summer and of spring;
Undeviating transience galore
That all must die, for Nature only brings
New life to that which dared to die before.

But death brings beauty even in its wake
With trees aflame in orange, yellow, red;
'Til winds and coming winter always take
The brilliance from the colors of the dead.

But barren trees and grey skies usher in
The purest white of winter's offering.
While darkened days, and long dark nights begin
A longing for the light and life of spring.

A time for life, a time for death, is not
A mere cliché, for seasons follow true.
But such yields much more meaningful the thought
That death serves but to resurrect the new.

I Know Why

2012-10-16

"I know why the caged bird sings,"
Penned poet Maya Angelou;
And while pursuing other things,
I think I may have learned why, too.

She sings because there is no cage
Preventing her eternal songs;
Her perch is but an opera stage
Of gilded wire. She merely longs

To sing the freedom of her heart.
No pen can silence Nature's score
Since every note is God-wrought art
Ne'er sung again, nor sung before.

And thus the cagèd bird sees past
Her false confinement, singing free
Her liberty, never surpassed,
In solitary symphony.

Untitled #22

2012-11-12

I'm floundering in shame and guilt
In heartache I don't understand.
In sin or not, perhaps I've built
A home inside the hourglass sand.

I must say, I was not aware
Of all the possibilities
When first I felt addiction's snare.
My body ached for time to freeze.

For now I faced the roughsome road
Of weaning off those pill-shaped asps;
The failings, feelings, to unload
What scraps of sanity I grasped.

I fault myself for this, since I
Knew somewhat of the risks I took;
I'm angry for each self-told lie
Spilled out to get me off the hook.

O, Butterfly, if ever I
Could use your name as sand pours down
Upon my head and in my eyes,
That precious moment would be now.

The God of Abraham

2012-11-19

In my mind's eye, God's throne room is the blueprint of the
    Lincoln Memorial
Except white.
All is dazzling, deafening white marble: pure, frozen, frigid.
Even God, in His Lincoln-ness, sits icy white. Motionless.
    Eyes set firm in a holy, blind, unblinking, blank
    stare—the Holy Maestro of the White-Silent
    Symphony.

Though standing at the doorway, yet to enter, I note the
    unmistakable cacophony of color—my color—
A dropped cymbal shattering the silent symphonic sacrament
    like so much glass on a flagged floor,
Blinding the code of holiness with my color-broken noise.
Anticipating the guaranteed glares from all who remain
    absent, I cower in shame and guilt
Only to discover that my clutter-clattered rainbow has drawn
    no attention at all—

For I belong not here.

I have mistaken holy for hueless
Righteous for lacking lustre
Sacred for static, stolid, solid, silent.

This is not the throne room of the Holy Prism.

The Sabbath Death

2012-11-27

I know I am an uninvited guest;
From birth I eat my fill of what you've sown.
How well I wear the moniker of "pest;"
Yet I hate what I am more than you've known.

I'm green or brown, with ample legs to spare;
Your garden is my happy hunting ground.
My goal is not to leave your garden bare,
Though I'm aware how hollow that must sound.

A worm with legs, antennae, appetite,
Consumed with food, by food, perhaps *as* food.
But on this day I'll take my final bite
And die alone, in sacred solitude.

I'm still and silent, shrouded in the black
Of what I know to be my final days.
My body starts to wither, shrivel, crack—
Yet I feel nothing as my form decays.

Then suddenly my coffin can't contain
My desiccated flesh a moment more;
It's rent from inside out—yet I remain
Alive, but not the way I was before.

Then light assaults my dark-familiar eye;
I crawl outside—surprised I did not die;
Unfold my wings, and leap to meet the sky:
A worm no more. I am a butterfly.

Untitled #23

2013

Of all the dreams I fantasize
Of ivory castles in the skies
Of buttercups and butterflies
Of all that never satisfies
I only want to make my Father smile.

In honest worship of His name
In carrying the Spirit's flame
Though holding on to guilt and shame
Believing I am much to blame
I only want to make my Father smile.

Through years of ceaseless health distress
Through murky, muddy mindlessness
Through strength I don't myself possess
Through endless sin I don't confess
I only want to make my Father smile.

As fear crowds out God-wrought virtue
As feelings drown out what is true
As fiercely as I push on through
As I protect my Me from you
I only want to make my Father smile.

Untitled #24

2013

Day after day after day after day
As I approach awakening
After an abnormally abundant absence of alertness
I already anticipate the antagonistic advantage to abort
    all attempts to
    achieve anything
    accomplish anything
Assuming an air of apathy
    in advance of the accepted apprehension of attention
Abdicating ahead of the actual attack
Abandoning any agenda
Acquiescing to affliction
    to avoid the affirmation of aimlessness
    the arrested aspiration of ambition.
Again. and Again.

Day after day after day after day
Distractions defy my Divine desires,
    disrupting my doubtless discernment
    discouraging my decreasingly distinct discretion by
    dividing my diligent devotion and direction into
    divergent, dubious drifting—
Devoid of definition.
Drawn downward, derailed, and
At Day's demise
Depleted.

Day after day after day after day
My failures flutter before my face—
    flood my focus until,
    like flesh-fed flies in the forest,
Forgiveness forfeits in favor of falsehood
    of the fault-filled fiction from
The forever-foiled Fiend.

Becoming One

2013-02-20

They wed with kilted fathers, friends, and groom.
A piper plays to greet, in Scots costume,
The treasury of souls who interlace
With theirs; a miracle of time and place.
Both bride and groom at peace, eager to share
The love and miracles that bring them there.
A joyous day to celebrate replete;
To pipes and drums the gallant ushers seat
The guests; while bride and father wait to hear
Their cue to enter; eyes with diamond tears.
Then guests arise as father, daughter stride;
In radiant whiteness, gown enhances bride—
Her tailor will she greet with gleaming smile,
For 'tis his gownèd bride come down the aisle.
With tearful joy the Daddy, child stand;
As with a kiss, she must release his hand.
He turns to face the one he will call "Son,"
And smiling, nods, to bless them now as one.

My God, My God

2013-02-26

"My God, My God, O why hast Thou
Forsaken Me?" we heard Him cry;
Not one of us could fathom how
God turned His back, and let Him die.

I couldn't move; so I reproached
Myself for trusting such a fool.
Had every hearer failed to broach
The lunacy that He could rule

Our people? This man was no king;
In poverty, though skilled in trade,
He lived off others' offering
While leading crowds in vast parades

Of desperate, dirty, damaged lives,
Whose confidence He swayed with words—
As one who easily contrives
Whatever draws the hopeless herds.

Then from the cross He met my eyes,
And held them 'til my knees gave way.
From what, I could not recognize—
No thing I knew, nor know today.

Then He was dead, and I cried now:
My God, my God, O why hast Thou

Forgiven me?

Psalm #1

2013-11-27

Praise the Lord, for He is good!
God is all the Yes in my heart!
He blessed me with abundant grace,
Unrelenting gifts of love, forgiveness, peace, and joy.
He demands all and nothing:
    All of my devotion, obedience, will;
    Nothing of my attempts to please Him.
For He has already claimed me as His own;
His Spirit is the only way I will grow.
Jesus, my Lord and my Savior, emptied Himself
Only to be filled with all that is unholy.
His emptiness was designed to become so full of evil
That He became Sin itself.
Praise our glorious Savior, whose great love
Reaches far beyond our slightest understanding!
Thank the One whose victory changed
The course of the cosmos, from beginning to end!
Live in the Yes that cannot be defied!
    Yes!

The Final Oath

2014-02-16

I pledge allegiance to the empty tomb
Of the One Who entered dead and exited alive,
And to the incomprehensible Love for which it stands;
One Divine sacrifice, forgiving all mankind,
With eternal salvation extended to all.

After Psalm 46:10a

Be still, and know that I Am God.
Be still   know   I Am God.
Be   know   God.

Stop moving, and remember who I Am.
Silence yourself, and concentrate on Me.
Hold still, and find where I Am in you.
Clear your thoughts, and replace them with Me.
Look up, and believe Who I Am.
Pause, and be aware of My Presence.
Stop working, and see My Work in you.
Forget your worries, and choose to trust Me instead.
Lose yourself in Me and discover True Freedom.
Inhale deeply, and feel MyFulness.
Close your eyes, and see My Smile upon you.
Step outside, and discover My Beauty within creation.
Empty your lungs, and breathe in My Life.
Sit still, and whisper My Name.
Relax, and discover that My Work is what matters.
Set aside your agenda, and follow Me through the day.
Stop the clock; find that time with Me accomplishes more.
Turn off your phone, and answer My Call.
Release your expectations, and wait expectantly on Me.
Let go of My Creation, and cling only to Me.
Receive My Blessings, and trust me to be your Sole Provider.
Wait, and I will show you Joy.
Leave illusions of control, and acknowledge My Greatness.
Slow down, so that I can become your True Lord.
Be simple, and let Me untangle you.
Stop fearing, and experience My Perfect Love.

Close your mouth, and listen to Me.
Linger for a moment. I will reveal Myself to you.
Come to a halt and give Me your full attention.
Blink, and return to seeing through My eyes.
Cease striving, and believe that I have chosen you.
I have done the work for you.
Stay where you are, and see Me in everything.
Quiet your heart, and accept My Peace.
Unplug your TV and see that I Am far more entertaining.
Shut down your computer; let Me connect you to the world.
Put down your pen, and receive all that I have in store.

Go!

Psalm #2

2014-03-11

God of all
  Owner of all
    Power over all
      Giver of all
        Essence of all
In a word, Love.
Where are you?

                    I Am in your pen
                 In the ink saturating the paper
           On which you express how I Am in your heart.

My heart. You are in my heart.

                           Everywhere you are.
In the air
  In my confusion
    In my joy
      In the thunder
        In the silence
Everywhere, You are.

Untitled #25

2014-05-14

I am learning to walk.
I have been flexing my chubby legs for months,
    Developing strength as a 1980s VHS workout:
    Deep knee bends and pull-ups.
We have practiced together, you and I,
Ten thick little fingers wrapped around two of yours,
    Arms high and "steps"—
    Movement initiated by your lead.
And I have practiced as well:
    Pulling myself to the coffee table—
    The one bearing numerous marks of my teething—
    Teaching my feet to flatten and my ankles to carry me.
Soon I will surprise myself by taking a single step away
Before I drop onto my diapered butt,
But I will keep trying until the day I release your fingers
And toddle to Papa.
But I will never let go of your hand.

Psalm #3

2014-09-07

Holy, almighty God,
My need for Your intervention is limitless.
I beg You,
    Give me a genuinely broken and contrite heart!
    Put Your holy eyes in mine
    So I can see that I am not
    The center of anything but my own selfish heart.
Teach me to forget Me
    And remember that
    I am tired of my story.
I want others to captivate me
    Until I get lost in everything that is
Not Me.

It Dawns on Me

2014

Only Your love never ceases, never changes, never fades
Though in the morning with the sun Your mercies rise
I need not wait for dawn to know that I have been remade
I need not wait for mourning for another chance to change

For a new day starts each time I blink my eyes

A Psalm of Awakening

2014-02-20

Wake up and say nothing until you have thought of the
Sovereign Lord, Who has created this day for you, a day
created for the First Time!
Rebuke all thoughts that are neither for nor of nor from
God.
Throw out the rotting rubbish you did not relinquish before
you sank into sleep, and be cleansed once more—
For this day has never been before,
Yet it has always been.
Time is only as real as it can be perceived, as God chooses to
reveal it.
Open your eyes to the first and only Today; prepare for it to
be invaded, interrupted, altered—acknowledge that
your every idea about this day is subject to the Divine
Scheduler,
Whose deepest desire is for you to know Him and relinquish
your day in grateful abandon.
Wake up! Make your first thought to be yielded to Him, your
first act to welcome your God into this day, which is
already His.
Allow yourself to awaken slowly, with intentional acceptance
and overwhelming relief that Today is no more yours
than the air you breathe.
Release each carefully scheduled moment of Today;
Leave each plan, appointment, task, fear, routine, and
expectation in the mighty hands of the One Who has
created every Today.

Release the captive sand of the hourglass—consider the basis
      of this ancient time-keeper: never full, never empty;
      always right-side-up-side-down with gravity as its
      only—but critical—necessity.
Feel the tiny grains of sand as they filter through your fingers:
Outside the hourglass, they have suddenly become
Meaningless.
Wake up! Open your eyes to the very First Today, and
      surrender it to your God;
For His Hands overflow with blessings that outnumber the
      grainy sands of ever-streaming moments.
Wake up!
Fill your lungs with anticipation and exhale all that is not God
      in a monumental sigh of sacrifice and relief,
For your God waits to fill your lungs, your Today, your soul,
      your sands. Your life!
Wake up, lest you miss the infinite blessings of your very first
Today!

www.ingramcontent.com/pod-product-compliance
Lightning Source LLC
Chambersburg PA
CBHW021011090426
42738CB00007B/746

* 9 7 8 0 9 7 8 7 5 5 4 7 8 *